INTRODUCTION

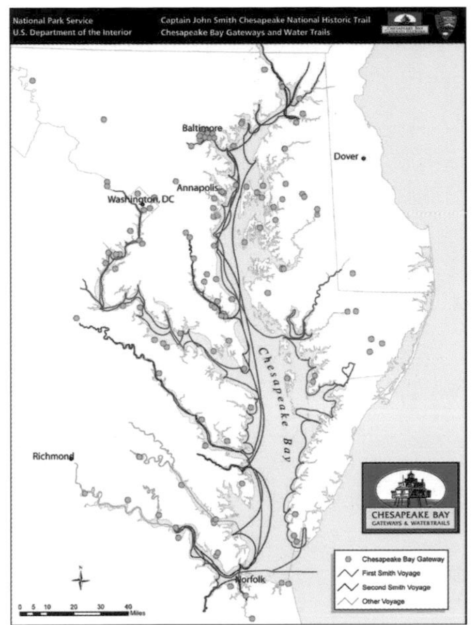

National Park Service
U.S. Department of the Interior
Captain John Smith Chesapeake National Historic Trail
Chesapeake Bay Gateways and Water Trails
Baltimore
Annapolis
Washington, DC
Dover
Richmond
Norfolk
CHESAPEAKE BAY

The Chesapeake Bay Gateways and Watertrails Network connects you with the Chesapeake Bay and its rivers through exceptional parks and water trails, wildlife refuges, museums, historic ships and communities, lighthouses and more. Enjoy these special places where you can experience the natural, cultural, and historical treasures of the authentic Chesapeake.

The Captain John Smith Chesapeake National Historic Trail commemorates the voyages of Captain Smith on the Chesapeake Bay and its tributaries in 1607-1609 in association with the founding of the first permanent British colony in North America at Jamestown. Accessible both by water and road, the trail also highlights 17th century American Indian towns and culture.

The Star-Spangled Banner National Historic Trail commemorates the Chesapeake Campaign of the War of 1812, culminating in the rebuff of the British in Baltimore and the writing of what became the National Anthem. The trail includes water and overland routes totaling 290 miles from Tangier Island at the south up to the head of the Bay.

To learn more about visiting Chesapeake Bay Gateways and Watertrails, the Captain John Smith Chesapeake National Historic Trail, and the Star-Spangled Banner National Historic Trail, visit ***FindYourChesapeake.com***.

The Chesapeake Conservancy supports the work of the National Park Service in the Chesapeake Bay watershed. Learn more at ***www.chesapeakeconservancy.org***.

Most illustrations show the adult male in breeding coloration. Colors and markings may be duller or absent during different seasons. The measurements denote the length of most animals from nose/bill to tail tip. Illustrations are not to scale.

Made in the USA

Waterford Press produces reference guides that introduce novices to nature, science, survival and outdoor recreation. Product information is featured on the website: **www.waterfordpress.com.**

Researched by Beverly McMillan.

Text and illustrations © 2011, 2019 by Waterford Press Inc. All rights reserved.

To order, call 800-434-2555.
For permissions, or to share comments, e-mail editor@waterfordpress.com.
For information on custom-published products, call 800-434-2555 or e-mail info@waterfordpress.com.

ISBN 978-1-58355-676-4
$7.95 U.S.
50795
9 781583 556764
UPC 8 84682 00890 1
10 9 8 7 6 5 4 3 2 1
902201

Chesapeake Bay Wildlife – An Introduction to Familiar Species

Chesapeake Bay Wildlife

An Introduction to Familiar Species

T0123953

a waterproof pocket guide

TREES

Red Maple
Acer rubrum To 90 ft. (27 m)
Leaves have 3-5 lobes and turn scarlet in autumn. Flowers are succeeded by red, winged seed pairs.

Atlantic White-cedar
Chamaecyparis thyoides To 90 ft. (27 m)
Slender twigs have opposite, scale-like leaves. Tiny cones grow to .25 in. (.6 cm) long.

American Holly
Ilex opaca To 70 ft. (21 m)
Tree or shrub is distinguished by its stiff, spiny evergreen leaves and red, poisonous berries.

Sweetbay Magnolia
Magnolia virginiana To 60 ft. (18 m)
Shiny, papery leaves are blunt-tipped. Cup-shaped flowers are fragrant.

Loblolly Pine
Pinus taeda To 100 ft. (30 m)
Long needles grow in bundles of 3. Oblong cones have scales armed with a curved spine.

White Oak
Quercus alba To 100 ft. (30 m)
Leaves have 7-9 prominent lobes. Acorn has a shallow, scaly cup.

Silver Maple
Acer saccharinum To 80 ft. (24 m)
Note short trunk and spreading crown. 5-lobed leaves are silvery beneath.

Flowering Dogwood
Cornus florida To 30 ft. (9 m)
Tiny flowers bloom in crowded clusters surrounded by 4 white petal-like structures.

Yellow Poplar
Liriodendron tulipifera To 120 ft. (36.5 m)
Note unusual leaf shape. Showy flowers are succeeded by cone-like aggregates of papery, winged seeds.

Black Tupelo
Nyssa sylvatica To 100 ft. (30 m)
Crown has horizontal branches. Glossy leaves turn red in autumn.

Virginia Pine
Pinus virginiana To 60 ft. (18 m)

Sassafras
Sassafras albidum To 60 ft. (18 m)
Aromatic tree or shrub has variously shaped leaves. Fruits are dark berries.

Baldcypress
Taxodium distichum To 120 ft. (36.5 m)
Note flaring trunk. Leaves are flattened and feathery. Protruding root 'knees' arise if growing in shallows.

WILDFLOWERS & FLOWERING SHRUBS

Wood Anemone
Anemone quinquefolia
To 8 in. (20 cm)
Found in moist meadows and woods.

Butterfly Weed
Asclepias tuberosa
To 3 ft. (90 cm)
Orange flowers are star-shaped.

Buttonbush
Cephalanthus occidentalis
To 10 ft. (3 m)
'Pincushion' flowers have protruding stamens.

Maryland Goldenaster
Chrysopsis mariana
To 2 ft. (60 cm)

Pink Moccasin Flower
Cypripedium acaule
To 14 in. (35 cm)

Mistflower
Conoclinium coelestinum
To 6 ft. (1.8 m)
Violet flowers are bell-shaped.

Joe-Pye Weed
Eupatorium maculatum
To 7 ft. (2.1 m)
Flowers are pink to purple. Leaves grow in whorls of 3-5.

Bottle Gentian
Gentiana clausa
To 2 ft. (60 cm)

Swamp Rose Mallow
Hibiscus moscheutos
To 6 ft. (1.8 m)
Large, rose-like flowers have petals that are pinkish on their inner edge.

Cardinal Flower
Lobelia cardinalis
To 4 ft. (1.2 m)

Indian Pipe
Monotropa uniflora
To 10 in. (25 cm)
Waxy white plant is parasitic on other plants in shady woods.

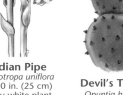

Devil's Tongue
Opuntia humifusa
To 12 in. (30 cm)
Clumps to 3 ft. (90 cm) wide.

WILDFLOWERS & FLOWERING SHRUBS

Mayapple
Podophyllum peltatum
To 18 in. (45 cm)
Cup-shaped flowers bloom between 2 leaves. Fruits are yellow.

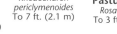

Orange Coneflower
Rudbeckia fulgida
To 2.5 ft. (75 cm)

Pink Azalea
Rhododendron periclymenoides
To 7 ft. (2.1 m)

Pasture Rose
Rosa carolina
To 3 ft. (90 cm)

Black-eyed Susan
Rudbeckia hirta
To 3 ft. (90 cm)
Flower has a dark, conical central disk.

Tall Goldenrod
Solidago altissima
To 7 ft. (2.1 m)

Common Blue Violet
Viola papilionacea
To 8 in. (20 cm)

AQUATIC/WETLAND PLANTS

Pickerelweed
Pontederia cordata
To 4 ft. (1.2 m)
Aquatic plant has dense spike of blue flowers.

Smooth Cordgrass
Spartina alterniflora
To 8 ft. (2.4 m)

Narrowleaf Cattail
Typha angustifolia
To 6 ft. (1.8 m)

Eelgrass
Zostera marina
To 4 ft. (1.2 m)
Grows beneath water surface.

MAMMALS ON LAND & IN THE BAY

American Beaver
Castor canadensis To 4 ft. (1.2 m)
Has a flat, paddle-like tail.

Virginia Opossum
Didelphis virginiana To 40 in. (1 m)
Note long fur and naked tail.

MAMMALS ON LAND & IN THE BAY

Northern River Otter
Lontra canadensis
To 52 in. (1.3 m)

Common Muskrat
Ondatra zibethicus To 2 ft. (60 cm)
Aquatic rodent has a naked tail that is flattened on its sides.

Eastern Cottontail
Sylvilagus floridanus
To 18 in. (45 cm)

Common Raccoon
Procyon lotor To 40 in. (1 m)

Eastern Gray Squirrel
Sciurus carolinensis
To 20 in. (50 cm)

White-tailed Deer
Odocoileus virginianus
To 7 ft. (2.1 m)
Fluffy tail is white below and held aloft when running.

Bobcat
Lynx rufus To 4 ft. (1.2 m)
Has dark lines on top of its 'bobbed' tail.

Gray Fox
Urocyon cinereoargenteus
To 3.5 ft. (1.1 m)
Note black-tipped tail.

Red Fox
Vulpes vulpes To 40 in. (1 m)
Note white-tipped tail.

Bottlenose Dolphin
Tursiops truncatus
To 12 ft. (3.6 m)

REPTILES & AMPHIBIANS

Eastern Box Turtle
Terrapene carolina carolina
To 9 in. (23 cm)
Note high-domed shell.

Loggerhead
Caretta caretta
To 4 ft. (1.2 m)
Brown shell is streamlined.

Snapping Turtle
Chelydra serpentina
To 18 in. (45 cm)
Note large head, knobby shell and long tail.

Eastern Painted Turtle
Chrysemys picta picta To 10 in. (25 cm)
Note red marks on outer edge of shell.

Black Rat Snake
Elaphe obsoleta obsoleta
To 8 ft. (2.4 m)

Diamondback Terrapin
Malaclemys terrapin
To 9 in. (23 cm)
Shell segments are deeply ridged.

Northern Water Snake
Nerodia sipedon To 4.5 ft. (1.4 m)
Note dark blotches on back.

Copperhead
Agkistrodon contortrix
To 52 in. (1.3 m)
Venomous snake has hourglass-shaped bands down its back.

Southeastern Five-lined Skink
Plestiodon inexpectatus To 9 in. (23 cm)
Smooth, glossy scales. Has five narrow light stripes down back.

Fowler's Toad
Anaxyrus woodhousii fowleri
To 5 in. (13 cm)

Eastern Fence Lizard
Sceloporus undulatus
To 8 in. (20 cm)
Rough scaled. Has dark, zigzag bars down its back.

Green Frog
Lithobates clamitans
To 4 in. (10 cm)
Single-note call is a banjo-like twang.

WATERFOWL & MARSH BIRDS

Mallard
Anas platyrhynchos To 28 in. (70 cm)

Ruddy Duck
Oxyura jamaicensis
To 16 in. (40 cm)

Canvasback
Aythya valisineria To 2 ft. (60 cm)

Bufflehead
Bucephala albeola To 15 in. (38 cm)

Hooded Merganser
Lophodytes cucullatus
To 20 in. (50 cm)

Wood Duck
Aix sponsa To 20 in. (50 cm)

Tundra Swan
Cygnus columbianus
To 4.5 ft. (1.4 m)

Canada Goose
Branta canadensis
To 43 in. (1.1 m)

Great Blue Heron
Ardea herodias
To 4.5 ft. (1.4 m)

Striated Heron
Butorides striata
To 14 in. (35 cm)
Note black cap.

Snowy Egret
Egretta thula
To 26 in. (65 cm)
Note black bill and yellow feet.

Herring Gull
Larus argentatus
To 26 in. (65 cm)
Note pink legs.

Laughing Gull
Leucophaeus atricilla
To 18 in. (40 cm)

Clapper Rail
Rallus longirostris
To 16 in. (40 cm)

SONGBIRDS, RAPTORS & OTHERS

Turkey Vulture
Cathartes aura
To 32 in. (80 cm)

Cooper's Hawk
Accipiter cooperii
To 20 in. (50 cm)

Red-tailed Hawk
Buteo jamaicensis
To 25 in. (63 cm)

Osprey
Pandion haliaetus
To 2 ft. (60 cm)

Bald Eagle
Haliaeetus leucocephalus
To 40 in. (1 m)

Barred Owl
Strix varia
To 2 ft. (60 cm)
Call is a rhythmic – who-cooks-for-you.

Eastern Screech-Owl
Megascops asio
To 9 in. (23 cm)

Ruby-throated Hummingbird
Archilochus colubris
To 3.5 in. (9 cm)

Wild Turkey
Meleagris gallopavo
To 4 ft. (1.2 m)

Pileated Woodpecker
Dryocopus pileatus
To 20 in. (50 cm)

Carolina Chickadee
Poecile carolinensis
To 4.5 in. (11 cm)

Carolina Wren
Thryothorus ludovicianus
To 6 in. (15 cm)

Eastern Bluebird
Sialia sialis
To 7 in. (18 cm)

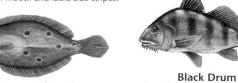

American Goldfinch
Spinus tristis
To 5 in. (13 cm)

Northern Cardinal
Cardinalis cardinalis
To 9 in. (23 cm)

FRESHWATER FISHES

White Catfish
Ameiurus catus To 2 ft. (60 cm)
Chin barbels are white. Often pot-bellied.

American Eel
Anguilla rostrata To 5 ft. (1.5 m)
Snake-like fish has long dorsal and anal fins.

Chain Pickerel
Esox niger To 31 in. (78 cm)
Has chain-like pattern on sides. Anadromous.

Pumpkinseed
Lepomis gibbosus To 16 in. (40 cm)

SALTWATER FISHES

Atlantic Sturgeon
Acipenser oxyrhynchus To 15 ft. (5 m)
Extinct except in James and York rivers.

Atlantic Menhaden
Brevoortia tyrannus To 18 in. (45 cm)

American Shad
Alosa sapidissima To 30 in. (75 cm)
Note line of spots behind gill cover.

Mummichog
Fundulus heteroclitus To 6 in. (15 cm)

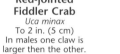
Spot
Leiostomus xanthurus To 14 in. (35 cm)
Note single spot on shoulder.

Atlantic Croaker
Micropogonias undulatus
To 2 ft. (60 cm)
Has 3-5 pairs of tiny barbels on chin.
Makes a croaking sound when excited.

White Perch
Morone americana To 22 in. (55 cm)
Has a small mouth and lacks side stripes.

Striped Bass
Morone saxatilis To 6 ft. (1.8 m)
Has 6-9 dark side stripes.

Summer Flounder
Paralichthys dentatus To 3 ft. (90 cm)

Black Drum
Pogonias cromis To 6 ft. (1.8 m)
Has prominent chin barbels.

AQUATIC INVERTEBRATES

Blue Crab
Callinectes sapidus
To 9 in. (23 cm)

Eastern Oyster
Crassostrea virginica
To 10 in. (25 cm)

Sea Nettle
Chrysaora quinquecirrha
To 10 in. (25 cm)

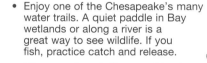
Atlantic Ribbed Mussel
Geukensia demissa
To 4 in. (10 cm)

Grass Shrimp
Palaemonetus pugio
To 2 in. (5 cm)

Northern Quahog
Mercenaria mercenaria
To 5 in. (13 cm)

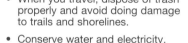
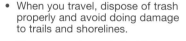
Common Periwinkle
Littorina littorea
To 1 in. (3 cm)

Red-jointed Fiddler Crab
Uca minax
To 2 in. (5 cm)
In males one claw is larger then the other.

Long-clawed Hermit Crab
Pagurus longicarpus
To 1 in. (3 cm)
Lives inside an empty snail shell.

INSECTS

Luna Moth
Actias luna
To 4.5 in. (11 cm)

Orb Weaver
Araneus spp.
To .75 in. (2 cm)

Monarch
Danaus plexippus
To 4 in. (10 cm)

Millipede
Order Diplopoda
To 5 in. (13 cm)
Has 2 pairs of legs per body segment.

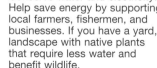
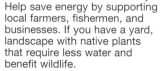

Cicada
Tibicen spp.
To 1.5 in. (4 cm)

Eastern Tiger Swallowtail
Papilio glaucus
To 6 in. (15 cm)

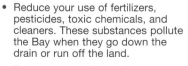
Black Widow Spider
Latrodectus mactans
To .5 in. (1.3 cm)
Female has a red hourglass marking on its abdomen. Venomous.

Praying Mantis
Mantis religiosa
To 2.5 in. (6 cm)
Front legs are held as if praying.

THE BAY AT A GLANCE

Chesapeake Bay is North America's largest estuary, a place where fresh water and sea water mingle.

Length: 180 miles, from northernmost Maryland to southernmost Virginia.

Major tributaries: Susquehanna, Potomac, Rappahannock, James, and York rivers.

Total watershed: 64,000 square miles, including parts of Pennsylvania, Maryland, West Virginia, Delaware, Washington, D.C., and New York.

Wildlife: More than 3,600 species of plants and animals.

Tautog

HELP PROTECT & RESTORE THE BAY

Chesapeake Bay today is beautiful and teeming with life, but harmful effects of pollution and other development-related pressures are mounting. Residents and visitors alike have a stake in restoring the Bay's health. To learn more about the Bay, its wildlife and ways you can help, visit the Chesapeake Bay Program web site at **www.chesapeakebay.net.**

Here are some simple things you can do to help.

- Visit Chesapeake Bay Gateways to learn about the natural, historical, and cultural heritage of the Bay region.

- Enjoy one of the Chesapeake's many water trails. A quiet paddle in Bay wetlands or along a river is a great way to see wildlife. If you fish, practice catch and release.

- When you travel, dispose of trash properly and avoid doing damage to trails and shorelines.

- Conserve water and electricity. Help save energy by supporting local farmers, fishermen, and businesses. If you have a yard, landscape with native plants that require less water and benefit wildlife.

- Reduce your use of fertilizers, pesticides, toxic chemicals, and cleaners. These substances pollute the Bay when they go down the drain or run off land.

- Support restoration and conservation efforts in the Bay watershed. Share your growing appreciation and concern about the Bay with family, friends, and neighbors.

Dragonfly

Red Beard Sponge

Horseshoe Crab

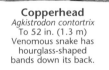